T0064982

POOR RICHARD'S
ALMANACK

POOR RICHARD'S ALMANACK

Benjamin Franklin

Introduction by
Paul A. Volcker

Skyhorse Publishing

Skyhorse Publishing books may be purchased in bulk
at special discounts for sales promotion, corporate gifts,
fund-raising, or educational purposes. Special editions
can also be created to specifications. For details, contact
the Special Sales Department, Skyhorse Publishing, 307
West 36th Street, 11th Floor, New York, NY 10018 or
info@skyhorsepublishing.com.

Skyhorse® and Skyhorse Publishing® are registered
trademarks of Skyhorse Publishing, Inc.®, a Delaware
corporation.

Visit our website at www.skyhorsepublishing.com.

Library of Congress Control Number: 2007936296

20 19 18 17 16 15 14 13

ISBN 13: 978-1-60239-117-8
ISBN 10: 1-60239-117-3

Printed in the United States of America

CONTENTS

INTRODUCTION

How does one write an introduction to something that has become so much a part of our common language? Early to bed, early to rise . . . Don't throw stones if you live . . . God helps those . . . A penny saved . . . No gain without . . . And on and on.

I don't know how many of these proverbs Ben Franklin made up himself back in Philadelphia in the mid-eighteenth century. For all I know, the Greeks and the Romans, maybe even the Egyptians, had their own versions. What I do know is that all these apothegms (now there's a fresh word for you) in *Poor Richard's Almanack* are fun to browse.

Some of them are, in fact, "terse and witty instructive sayings" (*The American Heritage Dictionary*, entry on "apothegms"). Some are dated: After all, a penny is hardly worth saving these days, even for a miser like me. Conversely, a fair number seem particularly apropos for today's world.For example: The magistrate should obey the laws. Sudden power is apt to be insolent, sudden liberty saucy. Pray, don't burn my house to roast your eggs.

To be sure, some seem strained, trite, even pointless. But that's a matter of taste. And to be expected considering there are nine hundred of them.

What I know for sure is that this book made Ben Franklin both famous and wealthy when it's first edition was published more than 250 years ago. It's fun to read in bits and pieces, just right for the bedside table or the guest room. You may even use it to introduce your kids to one of America's founders and to remind them that there are lessons about life that never change.

And it's just as handy and portable as the latest PlayStation!

Paul A. Volcker
January 10, 2007

POOR RICHARD'S
ALMANACK

ON MONEY AND BUSINESS

In Rivers and bad Governments, the lightest things swim at top.

Light purse, heavy heart.

Keep thy shop, and thy shop will keep thee.

Necessity never made a good bargain.

'Tis a well spent penny that saves a goat.

Drive thy Business, or it will drive thee.

Speak little, do much.

Ask and have, is sometimes dear buying.

The master's eye will do more work than both his hands.

He that sows thorns, should never go barefoot.

Ill Customs & bad Advice are seldom forgotten.

He that riseth late, must trot all day, and shall scarce overtake his business at night.

He that speaks ill of the Mare, will buy her.

A country man between two lawyers, is like a fish between two cats.

A large train makes a light purse.

After crosses and losses, men grow humbler and wiser.

There are three faithful friends—an old wife, an old dog, and ready money.

At the working man's house hunger looks in, but dares not enter.

A good lawyer, a bad neighbour.

He that would have a short Lent, let him borrow money to be repaid at Easter.

If Passion drives, let Reason hold the Reins.

You will be careful, if you are wise,
How you touch men's Religion, or Credit, or Eyes.

Money & Man a mutual Friendship show:
Man makes false Money, Money makes Man so.

Industry pays Debts, Despair encreases them.

There is much money given to be laught at, thought the purchasers don't know it; witness A's fine horse, and B's fine house.

The poor man must walk to get meat for his stomach, the rich man to get a stomach for his meat.

Avarice and happiness never saw each other; how then should they become acquainted?

The worst wheel of the cart makes the most noise.

The use of money is all the advantage there is in having money.

For 6£ a year you may have use of 100£, if you are a man of known prudence and honesty.

He that idly loses 5s. worth of time, loses 5s., and might as prudently throw 5s. into the river. He that loses 5s. not only loses that sum, but all the other advantages that might be made turning it in dealing, which, by the time a young man becomes old, amounts to a comfortable bag of money.

A penny saved is two pence clear. A pin a-day is a groat a-year. Save and have.

Every little makes a mickle.

If you'd be wealthy, think of saving, more than of getting: The Indies have not made Spain rich, because her Outgoes equal her Incomes.

He's gone, and forgot nothing but to say farewell to his creditors.

Who is rich? He that rejoices in his Portion.

The Devil wipes his Breech with poor Folks' Pride.

An open foe may prove a curse; but a pretended foe is worse.

Wealth is not his that has it, but his that enjoys it.

A little well-gotten will do us more good,
Than lordships and scepters by Rapine and Blood.

He that buys by the penny, maintains not only himself, but other people.

He that hath a Trade, hath an Estate.

Sloth (like Rust) consumes faster than Labour wears: the used Key is always bright.

Light Gains, heavy Purses.

Changing Countries or Beds, cures neither a bad Manager, nor a Fever.

As Pride increases, Fortune declines.

Neither trust, nor contend, nor lay wagers, nor lend; And you'll have peace to your Lives' end.

Pay what you owe, and what you're worth you'll know.

Little Strokes, Fell great Oaks.

A Person threatening to go to Law, was dissuaded from it by his Friend, who desired him to *consider*, for the Law was chargeable. I don't care, reply'd the other, I will not consider, I'll go to Law. Right, said his Friend, for if you go to law, I am sure you don't consider.

If you'd lose a troublesome Visitor, lend him money.

Industry, Perseverance, & Frugality, make Fortune yield.

The poor have little,—beggars none;
The rich too much—enough not one.

A Wolf eats sheep but now and then;
Ten thousands are devour'd by men.

Avoid dishonest gain: no price can recompence the pangs of vice.

Content makes poor men rich; Discontent makes rich Men poor.

Well done, is twice done.

Proclaim not all thou knowest, all thou owest, all thou hast, nor all thou can'st.

Great beauty, great strength, and great riches are really and truly of no greater use; a right heart exceeds all.

A light purse is a heavy curse.

Help, Hands; for I have no Lands.

No gains without pains.

A Man without ceremony has a need of great merit in its place.

The creditors are a superstitious sect, great observers of set days and times.

Great spenders are bad lenders.

He who multiplies Riches multiplies Cares.

The Eye of a Master, will do more Work than his Hand.

Beware of little Expenses: a small Leak will sink a great Ship.

Be always ashamed to catch thyself idle.

Poverty wants some things, luxury many things, avarice all things.

Old Boys have their Playthings as well as young Ones; the Difference is only in the Price.

Many have been ruined by buying good pennyworths.

When there's no Law, there's no Bread.

A rich rogue is like a fat dog, who never does good till as dead as a log.

He that lieth down with dogs, shall rise up with fleas.

Take counsel in wine, but resolve afterwards in water.

God works wonders now and then; Behold! a lawyer, an honest man.

He that drinks fast, pays slow.

Great famine when wolves eat wolves.

Beware of meat twice boil'd, and an old foe reconcil'd.

There is no little enemy.

When Prosperity was well mounted, she let go the Bridle, and soon came tumbling out of the Saddle.

He that waits upon fortune, is never sure of a dinner.

A fat kitchen, a lean will.

Would you persuade, speak of Interest, not of Reason.

A little House well fill'd, a little Field well till'd, and little Wife well will'd, are great riches.

Where carcasses are, eagles will gather; where good Laws are, much people flock thither.

Lawyers, preachers, and tomtit's eggs, there are more of them hatched than come to perfection.

All things are cheap to the saving, dear to the wasteful.

Nothing humbler than Ambition, when it is about to climb.

An innocent plowman is more worthy than a vicious prince.

He that is rich need not live sparingly, and he that can live sparingly need not be rich.

Virtue and a Trade, are a Child's best Portion.

Don't think to hunt two Hares with one Dog.

All things are easy to Industry, all things difficult to Sloth.

He that cannot obey, cannot command.

Laws like to cobwebs, catch small flies;
Great ones break through before your eyes.

An egg to-day is better than a hen to-morrow.

Drink water, put the money in your pocket, and leave
the dry-bellyache in the punch-bowl.

The magistrate should obey the laws, the people
should obey the magistrate.

Necessity has no law; I know some attorneys of the
same.

He does not possess wealth, it possesses him.

The thrifty maxim of the wary Dutch,
Is to save all the money they can touch.

By diligence and patience, the Mouse bit in two the
Cable.

'Tis against some Men's Principle to pay Interest, and
seems against others' Interest to pay the Principal.

The Good-will of the Govern'd will be starved, if not fed by the good deeds of the Governors.

Children and Princes will quarrel for trifles.

Success has ruin'd many a Man.

Haste makes Waste.

Early to bed and early to rise, makes a man healthy, wealthy, and wise.

To be humble to superiors is duty, to equals courtesy, to inferiors nobleness.

If you know how to spend less than you get, you have the philosopher's stone.

Diligence is the mother of good luck.

Wish a miser long life, and you wish him no good.

At a great penny worth, pause a while.

He that is of Opinion Money will do every Thing may well be suspected of doing every Thing for Money.

He that pays for work before it's done, has but a pennyworth for two pence.

A lean Award is better than a fat Judgment.

Patience in Market, is worth Pounds in a year.

When the well's dry, we know the worth of water.

A good Wife & Health, is a Man's best Wealth.

Buy what thou hast no need of, and e'er long thou shalt sell thy necessaries.

Sell not virtue to purchase wealth, nor liberty to purchase power.

He that sells upon trust, loses many friends, and always wants money.

Lovers, travellers, and poets, will give money to be heard.

Forewarn'd, forearm'd.

He that speaks much, is much mistaken.

Creditors have better memories than debtors.

Prosperity discovers Vice, Adversity, Virtue.

Many a Man would have been worse, if his Estate had been better.

I have never seen the Philosopher's stone that turns lead into gold, but I have known the pursuit of it turn a man's gold into lead.

Never intreat a Servant to dwell with thee.

He that can have patience can have what he will.

Now I have a sheep and a cow, every body bids me good-morrow.

God helps them that help themselves.

Three things are men most likely to be cheated in, a Horse, a Wig, and a Wife.

Poverty, Poetry, and new Titles of honour, make men ridiculous.

He that lives well is learned enough.

Most People return small Favours, acknowledge middling ones, and repay great ones with Ingratitude.

What will not *Lux'ry* taste? Earth, Sea, and Air,
Are daily ransack'd for the Bill of Fare.

Don't judge of Men's Wealth or Piety, by their Sunday Appearances.

For want of a Nail the Shoe is lost; for want of a Shoe the Horse is lost; for want of a Horse the Rider is lost.

The busy man has few idle Visitors; to the boiling Pot the Flies come not.

Calamity and Prosperity are the Touchstones of Integrity.

Kings have long Arms, but misfortune longer; let none think themselves out of her Reach.

Love, cough, and a smoke, can't well be hid.

If you'd have a servant that you like, serve yourself.

To whom thy secret thou dost tell,
To him thy freedom thou dost sell.

He that pursues two hares at once, does not catch one and lets t'other go.

Tell a miser he's rich and woman she's old, you'll get no money of one, nor kindness of t'other.

The sleeping Fox catches no poultry. Up! up!

Don't go to the doctor with every distemper, nor to the lawyer with every quarrel, nor to the pot for every thirst.

If your riches are yours, why don't you take them with you t'other World?

If worldly Goods cannot save me from Death, they ought not to hinder me of eternal Life.

Ambition often spends foolishly what Avarice had wickedly collected.

Great Estates may venture more;
Little Boats must keep near Shore.

Rather go to bed supperless than run in debt for a breakfast.

Bad Gains are true Losses.

God gives all Things to Industry.

Diligence overcomes Difficulties, Sloth makes them.

A Change of Fortune hurts a wise Man no more than a Change of the Moon.

Tim and his Handsaw are good in their Place,
Tho' not fit for preaching or shaving a face.

When Knaves betray each other, one can scarce be blamed or the other pitied.

Content is the Philosopher's Stone, that turns all it touches into Gold.

For Age and Want save while you may;
No morning Sun lasts a whole Day.

Where Sense is wanting, everything is wanting.

The hasty Bitch brings forth blind Puppies.

Two dry Stocks will burn a green One.

Praise little, dispraise less.

Don't think so much of your Cunning, as to forget other Men's: a Cunning Man is overmatched by a cunning Man and a Half.

You may give a Man an Office, but you cannot give him Discretion.

A Child thinks 20 Shillings and 20 Years can scarce ever be spent.

To be intimate with a foolish Friend, is like going to Bed to a Razor.

Prodigality of Time produces Poverty of Mind as well of Estate.

The first Mistake in public Business, is the going into it.

He that's content hath enough. He that complains hath too much.

Spare and have is better than spend and crave.

Employ thy time well, if thou meanest to gain leisure.

Lend money to an enemy, and thou'lt gain him; to a friend, and thou'lt lose him.

Rob not God, nor the Poor, lest thou ruin thyself; the Eagle snatcht a Coal from the Altar, but it fired her Nest.

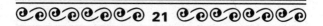

Wealth and Content are not always Bedfellows.

He that has a Trade has an Office of Profit and Honour.

The diligent Spinner has a large Shift.

A wise Man will desire no more than what he may get justly, use soberly, distribute chearfully and leave contentedly.

Pardoning the Bad, is injuring the Good.

Plough deep while Sluggards sleep; and you shall have Corn to sell and to keep.

Laziness travels so slowly that Poverty soon overtakes him.

He that by the Plough would thrive,
Himself must either hold or drive.

The generous Mind least regards Money and yet most feels the Want of it.

The second Vice is Lying; the first is running in Debt.

For one poor Man there are a hundred indigent.

A Plowman on his Legs is higher than a Gentleman on his Knees.

Pride breakfasted with Plenty, dined with Poverty, supped with Infamy.

Proportion your Charity to the strength of your Estate, or God will Proportion your Estate to the Weakness of your Charity.

The Borrower is a Slave to the Lender; the Security to both.

Where there is Hunger, Law is not regarded; and where Law is not regarded, there will be Hunger.

Think of three Things—whence you came, where you are going, and to Whom you must account.

There was never a good Knife made of bad Steel.

When a Friend deals with a Friend,
Let the bargain be clear and well penn'd,
That they may continue Friends to the End.

Get what you can, and what you get hold;
'Tis the Stone that will turn all your Lead into Gold.

An honest Man will receive neither Money nor Praise
that is not his due.

He that would rise at Court, must begin by creeping.

'Tis easier to build two Chimneys than maintain one
in Fuel.

He that would catch Fish, must venture his Bait.

Dally not with other Folks' Women or Money.

Work as if you were to live 100 years, Pray as if you
were to die To-morrow.

Idleness is the Dead Sea, that swallows all Virtues: Be
active in business, that Temptation may
miss her Aim; the Bird that sits, is easily shot.

Having been poor is no shame, but being ashamed of it, is.

Neither a fortress nor a maidenhead will hold out long after they begin to parley.

Hunger never saw bad bread.

The favour of the great is no inheritance.

Distrust and caution are the parents of security.

A fine genius in his own country, is like gold in the mine.

The old man has given all to his son: O fool! to undress thy self before thou art going to bed.

Where bread is wanting, all's to be sold.

There is neither honour nor gain, got in dealing with a villain.

Snowy winter, a plentiful harvest.

In success be moderate.

No man e'er was glorious, who was not laborious.

Hope of gain lessens pain.

Jack Little sow'd little, and little he'll reap.

Do good to thy friend to keep him, to thy enemy to gain him.

Bucephalus, the horse of Alexander, hath as lasting fame as his master.

When 'tis fair, be sure take your great coat with you.

Look before, or you'll find yourself behind.

Weighty questions ask for deliberate answers.

The king's cheese is half wasted in parings; but no matter, 'tis made of the peoples milk.

Nothing but money is sweeter than honey.

Opportunity is the great bawd.

He is no clown that drives the plow, but he that doth clownish things.

The good pay-master is lord of another man's purse.

Bargaining has neither friends nor relations.

When you are sick, what you like best is to be chosen for a medicine in the first place; what experience tells you is best, is to be chosen in the second place; what reason (i.e. theory) says is best, is to be chosen in the last place. But if you can get Dr. *Inclination*, Dr. *Experience*, and Dr. *Reason* to hold a consultation together, they will give you the best advice that can be taken.

God heals, and the doctor takes the fees.

If you desire many things, many things will seem but a few.

Receive before you write, but write before you pay.

The miser's cheese is wholesomest.

Don't misinform your doctor nor your lawyer.

'Tis less discredit to abridge petty charges, than to stoop to petty gettings.

Pollio, who values nothing that's within,
Buys books as men hunt beavers,—for their skin.

Industry need not wish.

O Lazy-bones! Dost thou think God would have given thee arms and legs, if he had not design'd thou should'st use them.

A cure for poetry,
Seven wealthy towns contend for *Homer,* dead,
Thro' which the living *Homer* beg'd his bread.

Some are justly laught at for keeping their money foolishly, others for spending it idly: he is the greatest fool that lays it out in a purchase of repentance.

When befriended, remember it: when you befriend, forget it.

Lying rides upon debt's back.

Rob not for burnt offerings.

No workman without tools,
Nor lawyer without fools,
Can live by their rules.

Money and good manners make the gentleman.

Death takes no bribes.

Beware, beware! He'll cheat 'ithout scruple, who can without fear.

Content and riches seldom meet together,
Riches take thou, contentment I had rather.

Speak in contempt of none, from slave to king,
The meanest bee hath, and will use, a sting.

If you'd have it done, go: if not, send.

Many a long dispute among divines may be thus abridg'd, It is so: It is not so, It is so; It is not so.

He who buys had need have 100 eyes, but one's enough for him that sells the stuff.

Women & wine,
Game & deceit,
Make the wealth small
And the wants great.

All mankind are beholden to him that is kind to the good.

Better is a little with content than much with contention.

He that's secure is not safe.

A cold April, the barn will fill.

Too much plenty makes mouth dainty.

Who dainties love, shall beggars prove.

A man has no more *goods* than he gets good by.

The art of getting riches consists very much in thrift. All men are not equally qualified for getting money, but it is in the power of every one alike to practise this virtue.

He that would be beforehand in the world, must be beforehand with his business: it is not only ill management, but discovers a slothful disposition, to do that in the afternoon, which should have been done in the morning.

Useful attainments in your minority will procure riches in maturity, of which writing and accounts are not the meanest.

'Tis hard (but glorious) to be poor and honest: an empty sack can hardly stand upright; but if it does, 'tis a stout one!

Those that have much business must have much pardon.

Bis dat qui cito dat: he gives twice that gives soon; i.e. he will soon be called upon to give again.

He that builds before he counts the cost, acts fool-ishly; and he that counts before he builds, finds he did not count wisely.

If you have no honey in your pot, have some in your mouth.

Gifts much expected, are *paid* not *given.*

The cat in gloves catches no mice.

If you'd know the value of money, go and borrow some.

The day is short, the work great, the workmen lazy, the wages high, the master urgeth; up, then, and be doing.

An hundred thieves cannot strip one naked man, especially if his skin's off.

Laws *too* gentle are seldom obeyed; *too severe*, seldom *executed*.

Trouble springs from *idleness*; toil from *ease*.

The way to be safe, is never be secure.

Great almsgiving, lessens no man's living.

To serve the publick faithfully, and at the same time please it entirely, is impracticable.

The idle man is the devil's hireling; whose livery is rags, whose diet and wages are famine and diseases.

Sleep without supping, and you'll rise without owing for it.

Have you somewhat to do to-morrow, do it today.

Lost time is never found again.

Idleness is the greatest Prodigality.

Many estates are spent in the getting,
Since women for tea forsook spinning and knitting.

Well done is better than well said.

ON LOVE, MARRIAGE, FAMILY, AND FRIENDSHIP

Be slow in chusing a friend, slower in changing.

No better relation that a prudent and faithful friend.

Ne'er take a wife till thou hast a house (and a fire) to put her in.

Monkeys, warm with envious spite,
Their most obliging friends will bite.

He that drinks his Cyder alone, let him catch his horse alone.

Tart Words make no Friends: a spoonful of honey will catch more flies than a Gallon of Vinegar.

Visit your Aunt, but not every Day; and call at your Brother's, but not every night.

Promises may get thee friends, but non-performance will turn them into enemies.

The same man cannot be both Friend and Flatterer.

A true Friend is the best Possession.

A Brother may not be a Friend, but a Friend will always be a Brother.

Hear no ill of a friend, nor speak any of an enemy.

If you would keep your secret from an enemy, tell it not to a friend.

A Father's a treasure; a Brother's a comfort; a Friend is both.

Friendship cannot live with Ceremony, nor without Civility.

Do good to they Friend to keep him, to thy Enemy to gain him.

Thou can'st not joke an enemy into a friend, but thou may'st a friend into an enemy.

Some Worth it argues, a Friend's Worth to know; Virtue to own the Virtue of a Foe.

'Tis better to leave an enemy at one's death, than beg of a friend in one's life.

Friendship increases by visiting Friends, but by visiting seldom.

The rotten apple spoils his companion.

'Tis great Confidence in a Friend to tell him your Faults, greater to tell him his.

Friends are the true Scepters of Princes.

A false Friend and a Shadow attend only while the Sun shines.

One good Husband is worth two good Wives; for the scarcer things are, the more they're valued.

Love and Lordship hate companions.

Fine linnen, girls and gold so bright,
Chuse not to take by candle light.

There are no ugly loves, nor handsome prisons.

He that goes far to marry, will either deceive or be deceived.

A ship under sail and a big-bellied woman, are the handsomest two things that can be seen common.

When ♂ and ♀ in conjunction lie,
Then, maids, whate'er is ask'd of you, deny.

Let thy maid-servant be faithful, strong, and homely.

Late Children, early Orphans.

Quarrels never could last long, if on one side lay the wrong.

He that has not got a Wife, is not yet a compleat Man.

Marry above thy match, and thou'lt get a master.

You can bear your own Faults, and why not a Fault in your Wife.

EPITAPH ON A SCOLDING WIFE BY HER HUSBAND

Here my poor Bridget's Corps doth lie,
She is at rest,—and so am I.

When man and woman die, as poets sung,
His heart's the last part moves, her last, the tongue.

Where there's marriage without love, there will be love without marriage.

An undutiful Daughter, will prove an unmanageable Wife.

After three days men grow weary of a wench, a guest, and weather rainy.

You cannot pluck roses without fear of thorns,
Nor enjoy a fair wife without danger of horns.

A good wife lost, is God's gift lost.

A man without a wife, is but half a man.

If you would be loved, love and be lovable.

Happy's the wooing that's not long a doing.

He that takes a wife takes Care.

A house without woman and firelight, is like a body without soul or sprite.

Beauty and folly are old companions.

Light heel'd mothers make leaden-heel'd daughters.

If you want a neat wife, go chuse her on a Saturday.

Keep your eyes wide open before marriage, half shut afterwards.

Why does the blind man's wife paint herself?

Love and Tooth-ache have many Cures, but none infallible, except Possession and Dispossession.

If Jack's in love, he's no Judge of Jill's Beauty.

Honour thy father and mother, i.e., live so as to be an honour to them tho' they are dead.

Let our fathers and grandfathers be valued for *their* goodness, ourselves for our own.

If you'd be belov'd, make yourself amiable.

'Tis a shame that your family is an honour to you! You ought to be an honour to your family.

Love, and be *loved*.

Teach your child to hold his tongue, he'll learn fast enough to speak.

The good or ill hap of a good or ill life,
is the good or ill choice of a good or ill wife.

Let thy child's first lesson be obedience, and the second will be what thou wilt.

An old Man in a House is a good Sign.

The proof of gold is fire; the proof of woman, gold; the proof of man, a woman.

ON HEALTH

There are more old Drunkards than old Doctors.

Give me yesterday's Bread, this Day's Flesh, and last Year's Cyder.

A full Belly makes a dull Brain.

Many Dishes, many Diseases.

Beware of the young doctor and the old barber.

Onions can make ev'n heirs and widows weep.

An infallible remedy for *toothache,* viz.—Wash the root of an aching tooth, in *Elder vinegar,* and let it dry half an hour in the sun; after which it will never ache more.

Poor Dick eats like a well man, and drinks like a sick.

Eat few Suppers, and you'll need few Medicines.

Cheese and salt meat should be sparingly eat.

It is ill Jesting with the Joiner's Tools, worse with the Doctor's.

After Fish, Milk do not wish.

Fear not death; for the sooner we die, the longer shall we be immortal.

There are lazy minds as well as lazy bodies.

Wish not so much to live long, as to live well.

He that spills the Rum loses that only; He that drinks it, often loses both that and himself.

Dine with little, sup with less: Do better still: sleep supperless.

A full Belly is the Mother of all Evil.

Wars bring scars.

Eat to live; live not to eat.

To lengthen thy life, lessen thy meals.

Keep your mouth wet, feet dry.

We are not so sensible of the greatest Health as of the least Sickness.

He's the best physician that knows the worthlessness of the most medicines.

Be temperate in wine, in eating, girls, and cloth, or the Gout will seize you and plague you both.

An old young man will be a young old man.

If thou would'st live long, live well; for folly and wickedness shorten life.

Time is an herb that cures all diseases.

I saw few die of hunger; of eating—100,000.

He that would travel much, should eat little.

The Muses starve in a Cook's Shop.

Pride and Gout are seldom cur'd throughout.

He's a fool that makes his doctor his heir.

Many medicines, few cures.

Pain wastes the body; pleasures the understanding.

He that can take rest is greater than he that can take cities.

RULES OF HEALTH AND LONG LIFE, ETC.

Eat and drink such an exact quantity as the constitution of thy body allows of, in reference to the services of the mind.

They that study much, ought not to eat so much as those that work hard, their digestion being not so good.

The exact quantity and quality being found out, is to be kept to constantly.

Excess in all other things whatever, as well as in meat and drink, is also to be avoided.

Youth, age, and sick require a different quantity.

And so do those of contrary complexions; for that which is too much for a flegmatick man, is not sufficient for a cholerick.

The measure of food ought to be (as much as possibly may be) exactly proportionable to the quality and condition of the stomach, because the stomach digests it.

That quantity that is sufficient, the stomach can perfectly concoct and digest, and it sufficeth the due nourishment of the body.

A greater quantity of some things may be eaten than of others, some being of lighter§ digestion than others.

The difficulty lies, in finding out an exact measure; but eat for necessity, not pleasure, for lust knows not where necessity ends.

Wouldst thou enjoy a long life, a healthy body, and a vigorous mind, and be acquainted also with the woderful works of God? Labour in the first place to bring thy appetite into subjection to reason.

RULES TO FIND OUT A FIT MEASURE OF MEAT AND DRINK

If thou eatest so much as makes thee unfit for study, or other business, thou exceedest the due measure.

If thou art dull and heavy after meat, it's a sign thou hast exceeded the due measure; for meat and drink ought to refresh the body, and make it chearful, and not to dull and oppress it.

If thou findest these ill symptoms, consider whether too much meat, or too much drink occasions it, or both, and abate little and little, till though findest the inconveniency removed.

Keep out of the sight of feasts and banquets as much as may be; for 'tis more difficult to refrain good cheer, when it's present, than from the desire of it when it is away; the like you may observe in the objects of all the other senses.

If a man casually exceeds, let him fast the next meal, and all may be well again, provided it be not too often done; as if he exceed at dinner, let him refrain a supper, &c.

A temperate diet frees from diseases; such are seldom ill, but if they are surprised with sickness, they bear it better, and recover sooner; for most distempers have their original for repletion.

Use now and then a little exercise a quarter of an hour before meals, as to swing a weight, or swing your arms about with a small weight in each hand; to leap, or the like, for that stirs the muscles of the breast.

A temperate diet arms the body against all external accidents; so that they are not so easily hurt but heat, cold or labour; if they at any time should be prejudiced, they are more easily cured, either of wounds, dislocations or bruises.

But when malignant fevers are rife in the country or city where thou dwelst, 'tis adviseable to eat and drink more freely, by way of prevention; for those are diseases that are not caused by repletion, and seldom attack full-feeders.

A sober diet makes a Man diet without pain; it maintains the senses in vigour; it mitigates the violence of passions and affections. It preserves the memory, it helps the understanding, it allays the heat of lust; it brings a man to a consideration of his latter end; it makes the body a fit tabernacle for the Lord to dwell in; which makes us happy in this world, and eternally happy in the word to come, through Jesus Christ our Lord and Saviour.

Nine men in ten are suicides.

ON HUMAN NATURE

The family of Fools is ancient.

The tongue offends, and the ears get the cuffing.

Three may keep a secret, if two of them are dead.

There's many witty men whose brains can't fit their bellies.

Who has deceiv'd thee so oft as thy self?

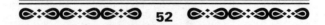

He that can travel well afoot, keeps a good horse.

A traveller should have a hog's nose, a deer's legs, and an ass's back.

Hope and a Red-Rag, are Baits for Men and Mackerel.

Anger warms the invention but overheats the oven.

They who have nothing to trouble them, will be troubled at nothing.

Declaiming against Pride, is not always a sign of Humility.

Neglect kills Injuries, Revenge increases them.

Great Good-nature, without Prudence, is a great Misfortune.

Do me the favour to deny me at once.

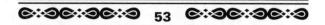

Eat to please thyself, but dress to please others.

He that would live in peace and at ease,
Must not speak all he knows, nor judge all he sees.

If you would have guests merry with cheer,
Be so yourself, or so at least appear.

Let all Men know thee, but no man know thee thoroughly: Men freely ford that see the shallows.

Ah simple Man! when a boy two precious jewels were given thee, Time and good Advice; one thou hast lost, and the other thrown away.

When Knaves fall out, honest men get their goods: When Priests dispute, we come at the Truth.

Speak and speed: the close mouth catches no flies.

Half Wits talk much but say little.

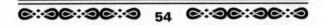
'Tis easy to see, hard to foresee.

In a discreet man's mouth a publick thing is private.

Here comes Courage! that seized the lion absent, and ran away from the present mouse.

Caesar did not merit the triumphal car more than he that conquers himself.

Nor eye in a letter, nor hand in a purse, nor ear in the secret of another.

Great talkers should be cropp'd, for they have no need of ears.

Those who in quarrels interpose, must often wipe a bloody nose.

Where yet was ever found their mother,
Who'd change her booby for another?

There are no fools so troublesome as those that have wit.

What you would seem to be, be really.

Hear Reason, or she'll make you feel her.

Make haste slowly.

What's proper is becoming: See the Blacksmith with his white Silk Apron!

The Morning Daylight appears plainer when you put out your Candle.

The Muses love the Morning.

Thirst after desert—not reward.

What is a Butterfly?—at best he's but a caterpillar drest.—The gaudy Fop's his picture just.

Tricks and treachery are the practice of fools that have not wit enough to be honest.

Who says Jack is not generous?—he is always fond of giving, and cares not for receiving,—what?—why, *advice*.

When you speak to a man, look on his eyes; when he speaks to thee, look on his mouth.

Observe all men; thyself most.

If any man flatters me, I'll flatter him again, though he were my best friend.

If you have time, don't wait for time.

There's none deceived but he that trusts.

None but the well-bred man knows how to confess a fault, or acknowledge himself in an error.

There is much difference between imitating a good man, and counterfeiting him.

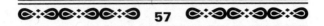

Wink at small faults—remember thou hast great ones.

To all apparent beauties blind, each blemish strikes an
envious mind.

A man of knowledge like a rich soil, feeds
If not a world of corn, a world of weeds.

Thou hadst better eat salt with the philosophers of
Greece, than sugar with the courtiers of Italy.

None are deceived, but they that confide.

No wonder Tom grows fat: th'unwieldly sinner
Makes his whole life but one continual dinner.

Enjoy the present hour, be mindful of the past;
And neither fear nor wish the approaches of the
last.

Many Foxes grow grey, but few grow good.

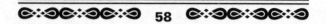

If your head is wax, don't walk in the Sun.

Petty & Witty will wound if they hit ye.

You may be too cunning for One, but not for All.

Many would live by their Wits, but break for want of stock.

Hide not your Talents, they for Use were made: What's a Sun-Dial in the Shade?

What signifies knowing the Names, if you know not the Natures of Things?

Death takes no bribes.

Anger and folly walk cheek by jole; repentance treads on both their heels.

There are three Things extreamly hard: Steel, a Diamond and to know oneself.

Pride is as loud a Beggar as Want, and a great deal more saucy.

If evils come not, then our fears are vain;
And if they do, fear but augments the pain.

Be not niggardly of what costs thee nothing, as courtesy, counsel, and countenance.

Man's tongue is soft, and bone doth lack;
Yet a stroke therewith may break a man's back.

To bear other people's afflictions, every one has courage and enough to spare.

All blood is alike ancient.

Those who are fear'd, are hated.

Let thy discontents be thy secrets;—if the world knows them 'twill despise thee and increase them.

Nick's passions grow fat and hearty: his understanding looks consumptive!

A lie stands on one leg, truth on two.

Great wits jump, says the poet, and hit his head against the post.

Ceremony is not Civility; nor Civility Ceremony.

Graft good fruit all, or graft not at all.

Many complain of their Memory, few of their Judgment.

A soft Tongue may strike hard.

You may talk too much on the best of subjects.

Don't overload gratitude; if you do, she'll kick.

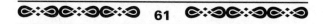

At 20 years old, the will reigns; at 30 the wit; at 40 the judgment.

What's given shines, what's receiv'd is rusty.

Mankind are very odd Creatures: One Half censure what they practice, the other half practice what they censure; the rest always say and do as they ought.

Great Merit is coy, as well as great Pride.

Hold your Council before Dinner; the full Belly hates thinking as well as Acting.

Praise to the undeserving, is severe Satyr.

He is not well bred, that cannot bear Ill-Breeding in others.

Kings and bears often worry their keepers.

Great talkers, little doers.

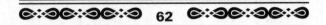

After feasts made, the maker scratches his head.

Doors and walls are fools' paper.

He has lost his boots, but sav'd his spurs.

Men and melons are hard to know.

Craft must be at charge for clothes, but Truth can go naked.

Write Injuries in Dust, Benefits in Marble.

A Slip of the Foot you may soon recover, but a slip of the Tongue you may never get over.

Cut the Wings of your Hens and Hopes, lest they lead you a weary Dance after them.

The Horse thinks one thing, and he that saddles him another.

Love your Neighbour; yet don't pull down your Hedge.

Tongue double, brings Trouble.

Would you live with ease, do what you ought, and not what you please.

People who are wrapped up in themselves make small packages.

If you ride a horse, sit close and tight,
If you ride a man, sit easy and light.

A pair of good Ears will drink dry an hundred Tongues.

Bite a man, and test his metal.

Full of courtesie, full of craft.

Approve not of him who commends all you say.

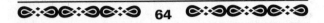

The discontented Man finds no easy Chair.

Take heed of the Vinegar of sweet Wine, and the Anger of Good-nature.

You may delay, but Time will not.

Despair ruins some, Presumption many.

Presumption first blinds a Man, then sets him a running.

Blame-all and Praise-all are two blockheads.

What one relishes, nourishes.

Never spare the parson's wine, nor the baker's pudding.

A great Talker may be no Fool, but he is one that relies on him.

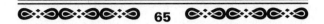

When Reason preaches, if you don't hear her she'll box your Ears.

Fools multiply folly.

Paintings and Fightings are best seen at a distance.

If you would reap Praise you must sow the Seeds, gentle Words and useful Deeds.

Sudden Pow'r is apt to be insolent, Sudden Liberty saucy; that behaves best which has grown gradually.

If man could have Half his Wishes, he would double his Troubles.

Philosophy as well as Foppery often changes Fashion.

Ever since follies have pleased, fools have been able to divert.

Here comes the orator, with his flood of words, and his drop of reason.

Sally laughs at everything you say. Why? Because she has fine teeth.

Do not do that which you would not have known.

When death puts out our flame, the snuff will tell, if we are wax, or tallow, by the smell.

Ignorance leads Men into a party, and Shame keeps them from getting out again.

Trust thyself, and another shall not betray thee.

Anger is never without a Reason, but seldom with a good One.

He that falls in love with himself, will have no rivals.

Grace thou thy house, and let not that grace thee.

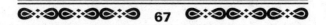

He that best understands the World, least likes it.

One Man may be more cunning than another, but not more cunning than every body else.

The Sting of a Reproach is the Truth of it.

An Ounce of wit that is bought,
Is worth a Pound that is taught.

He that resolves to mend hereafter, resolves not to mend now.

An ill Wound, but not an ill Name, may be healed.

He that Whines for Glass without G, take away L and that's he.

A quarrelsome Man has no good Neighbours.

Nothing brings more pain than too much pleasure; nothing brings more bondages than too much liberty, (or libertinism).

Read much, but not too many books.

You may be more happy than princes, if you will be more virtuous.

If you would not be forgotten, as soon as you are dead and rotten, either write things worth reading, or do things worth the writing.

Mary's mouth costs her nothing, for she never opens it but at others' expence.

Don't throw Stones at your Neighbours', if your own Windows are Glass.

Many a Man thinks he is buying Pleasure, when he is really selling himself a Slave to it.

Honest Tom! You may trust him with a house full of untold Millstones.

There is no Man so bad but he secretly respects the Good.

Glass, China, and Reputation, are easily crack'd, and never well mended.

Pray don't burn my House to roast your Eggs.

We must give Advice, but we cannot give Conduct.

Fly pleasures, and they'll follow you.

Since thou are not sure of a Minute, throw not away an Hour.

Since I cannot govern my own Tongue tho' within my own teeth, how can I hope to govern the Tongues of others?

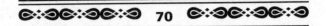

As we must account for every idle Word, so we must for every idle Silence.

If you do what you should not, you must hear what you would not.

Never praise your cider or your horse.

Reading makes a full man, Meditation a profound man, Discourse a clear man.

The Golden Age never was the present Age.

Nice Eaters seldom meet with a good Dinner.

Youth is pert and positive, Age modest and doubting: So Ears of Corn when young and light, stand bold upright, but hang their Heads when weighty, fully, and ripe.

'Tis easier to suppress the first Desire, than to satisfy all that follow it.

Drunkenness, that worst of Evils, makes some men Fools, some Beasts, some Devils.

Three good meals a day is bad living.

Is there anything men take more pains about than to make themselves unhappy?

Cunning proceeds from Want of Capacity.

Let thy Discontents be Secrets.

'Tis easier to prevent bad habits than to break them.

Blessed is he that expects nothing, for he shall never be disappointed.

When you taste Honey, remember Gall.

Neglect mending a small Fault, and 'twill soon be a great One.

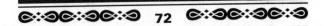

Beware of him that is slow to anger: He is angry for something, and will not be pleased for nothing.

Many a meal is lost for want of meat.

Love your Enemies, for they tell you your Faults.

Dost thou love Life? Then do not squander Time; for that's the Stuff Life is made of.

'Tis a strange Forest that has no rotten Wood in't
And a strange Kindred that all are good in't.

Mad Kings and mad Bulls are not to be held by treaties and packthread.

When there's more Malice shown than Matter:
On the Writer falls the Satyr.

When you're an Anvil, hold you still;
When you're a Hammer, strike your fill.

Mine is better than Ours.

He that hath no Ill-Fortune will be troubled with Good.

When the Wine enters, out goes the Truth.

Little Rogues easily become great Ones.

You may sometimes be much in the wrong, in owning your being in the right.

Good-Will, like the Wind, bloweth where it listeth.

The Honestly is sweet, but the Bee has a Sting.

Half Hospitality opens his Door and shuts up his Countenance.

A flatterer never seems absurd:
The flatter'd always takes his word.

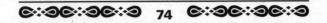

Willows are weak, but they bind the Faggot.

He makes a Foe, who makes a Jest.

Suspicion may be no fault, but showing it may be a great one.

Words may shew a man's Wit, but Actions his Meaning.

Vain-glory flowereth, but beareth no Fruit.

Be civil to all; sociable to many; familiar with few; Friend to one; Enemy to none.

To-morrow every Fault is to be amended; but that To-morrow never comes.

Knaves & Nettles are akin; stroak 'em kindly, yet they'll sting.

Wide will wear, but narrow will tear.

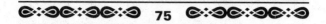

Silks and sattins put out the kitchen fire.

The Royal Crown cures not the Head-ache.

Shame and the Dry-belly-ache were Diseases of the last Age, this seems to be cured of them.

Act uprightly and despise Calumny; Dirt may stick to a Mud Wall, but not to polish'd Marble.

Singularity in the right, hath ruined many: happy those who are convinced of the general Opinion.

Tho' the Mastiff be gentle, yet bite him not by the Lip.

Most fools think they are only ignorant.

Tell me my Faults, and mend your own.

The Wolf sheds his Coat once a Year, his Disposition never.

The honest Man takes Pains, and then enjoys Pleasures; the knave takes Pleasure, and then suffers Pains.

Samson, for all his strong Body, had a weak Head, or he would not have laid it in a Harlot's lap.

He that never eats too much, will never be lazy.

To be proud of Knowledge, is to be blind with Light.

Men take more pains to mask than mend.

It is Ill-manners to silence a Fool, and Cruelty to let him go on.

All would live long, but none would be old.

Nothing dries sooner than a Tear.

If it were not for the Belly, the Back might wear Gold.

One To-day is worth two To-morrows.

Drink does not drown Care, but waters it, and makes it grow faster.

A life of leisure and a life of laziness are two things.

A man in a passion rides a mad horse.

Visits should be short, like a winter's day,
Lest you're too troublesome hasten away.

He has chang'd his one ey'd horse for a blind one.

Anoint a villain and he'll stab you, stab him, and he'll anoint you.

Nothing more like a fool, than a drunken man.

What pains our justice takes his faults to hide,
With half that pain sure he might cure 'em quite.

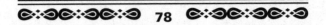

What e'er's begun in anger, ends in shame.

A new truth is a truth, and old error is an error, tho' Clodpate won't allow either.

As charms are nonsense, nonsense is a charm.

If you would be reveng'd of your enemy, govern yourself.

Great ones break through before your eyes.

Strange, that he who lives by shifts, can seldom shift himself.

As sore places meet most rubs, proud folks meet most affronts.

Bad commentators spoil the best of books,
So God sends meat, (they say,) the devil cooks.

Some are weatherwise, some are otherwise.

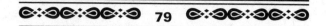

If pride leads the van, beggary brings up the rear.

There's small revenge in words, but words may be greatly revenged.

A man is never so ridiculous by those qualities that are his own, as by those that he affects to have.

Are you angry that others disappoint you? Remember you cannot depend upon yourself.

One mend-fault is worth two find-faults, but one find-fault is better than two make-faults.

He that has neither fools, whores nor beggars among his kindred, is the son of a thundergust.

Admiration is the daughter of ignorance.

The absent are never without fault, nor the present without excuse.

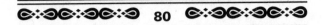

Gifts burst rocks.

If wind blows on you thro' a hole,
Make your will and take care of your soul.

Forewarn'd, forearm'd, unless in the case of cuckolds,
who are often forearm'd before warn'd.

The nearest way to come at glory, is to do that for
conscience which we do for glory.

Defer not thy well doing; be not like St. *George*, who
is always a horseback, and never rides on.

Historians relate, not so much what is done, as what
they would have believed.

No longer virtuous, no longer free; is a maxim as true
with regard to a private person as a commonwealth.

A——, they say, has wit; for what?
For writing?——No; for writing not.

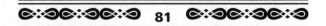

Who knows a fool, must know his brother;
For one will recommend another.

Neither praise nor dispraise, till seven Christmases be
over.

No wood without bark.

Joke went out and brought home his fellow, and they
two began a quarrel.

Up, sluggard, and waste not life; in the grave will be
sleeping enough.

Honours change manners.

Ben beats his pate, and fancys wit will come;
But he may knock, there's no body at home.

Tom, vain's your pains; they all will fail:
Ne'er was good arrow made of a sow's tail.

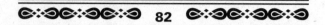

Ill company is like a dog who dirts those most, that he loves best.

The world is full of fools and faint hearts; and yet everyone has courage enough to bear the misfortunes, and wisdom enough to manage the affairs of his neighbour.

I'll warrant ye, goes before rashness; Who'd-a-tho't comes sneaking after.

It's common for men to give pretended reasons instead of one real one.

Had I revenged wrong, I had not worn my skirts so long.

Every man has assurance enough to boast of his honesty, few of their understanding.

Interest which blinds some People, enlighten others.

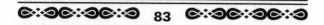

It's the easiest thing in the world for a man to deceive himself.

Good sense is a thing all need, few have, and none think they want.

The tongue is ever turning the aching tooth.

Want of care does us more damage than want of knowledge.

Take courage mortal; death can't banish thee out of the universe.

Strive to be the *greatest* man in your country, and you may be disappointed; strive to be the best, and you may succeed: he may well win the race that runs by himself.

None know the unfortunate, and the fortunate do not know themselves.

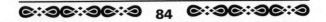

There's a time to wink as well as to see.

Courage would fight, but *discretion* won't let him.

What signifies your Patience, if you can't find it when you want it.

Time enough always proves *little enough*.

A mob's a monster; heads enough, but no brains.

He that cannot bear with other people's passions, cannot govern his own.

Welcome, mischief, if thou comest alone.

'Tis a laudable ambition, that aims at being better than his neighbors.

Fond pride of dress is sure an empty curse;
E're *fancy* you consult, consult your *purse*.

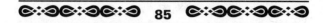

To-day is yesterday's pupil.

Who judges best of a man, his enemies or himself?

The prodigal generally does more injustice than the covetous.

A temper to bear much, will have much to bear.

The too obliging temper is evermore disobliging itself.

Setting too good an example is a kind of slander seldom forgiven; 'tis *scandalum magnatum.*

When out of favour, none know thee; when in, thou dost not know thyself.

Some make conscience of wearing a hat in church, who make none of robbing the altar.

The wit of conversation consists more in finding it in others, than shewing a great deal yourself. He

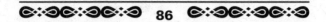

who goes out of your company pleased with his own facetiousness and ingenunity, will the sooner come into it again. Most men had rather *please* than *admire* you and seek less to be *instructed* and *diverted*, than *approved* and *applauded*; and it is certainly the most delicate sort of pleasure, to please another. But that sort of wit, which employs itself insolently in criticizing and censuring the words and sentiments of others in conversation, is absolute *folly*; for it answers none of the ends of conversation. He who uses it neither *improves others*, is *improved* himself, or *pleases* any one.

There is really a great difference in *things* sometimes where there seems to be but little distinction in *names*. The *man* of honour is an internal, the *person* of honour an external, the one a real, the other a fictitious, character. A *person* of honour may be a profane libertine, penurious, proud, may insult his inferiors, and defraud his creditors; but it is impossible for a *man* of honour to be guilty of any of these. The *person* of honour may flatter for court favours, or cringe for popularity; he may be for or against his country's good as it suits his private views. But the *man* of honour can do none of these.

Saying and *doing* have quarrel'd and parted.

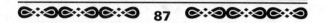

Many a man's own tongue gives evidence against his understanding

Happy Tom Crump, ne'er see his own hump.

Great modesty often hides great merit.

In a corrupt age, the putting the world in order would breed confusion; then e'en mind your own business.

Men often *mistake* themselves, seldom *forget* themselves.

Men meet, Mountains never.

Fish and Visitors stink after three days.

How few there are who have courage enough to own their Faults, or resolution enough to mend them!

ON VIRTUE, VICE, GOD, AND FAITH

Men differ daily, about things which are subject to sense, is it likely then they should agree about things invisible?

Serving God is doing good to Man, but praying is thought an easier Service, and therefore more generally chosen.

What maintains one Vice would bring up two children.

He is ill clothed that is bare of virtue.

The Proud hate Pride—in others.

Sam's religion is like a Cheder cheese, 'tis made of the milk of one-and-twenty parishes.

A good Example is the best Sermon.

It is observable that God has often called men to places of dignity and honour, when they have been busy in the honest employment of their vocation. *Saul* was seeking his father's asses, and *David* keeping his father's sheep, when called to the kingdom. The shepherds were feeding their flocks, when they had their glorious revelation. God called the four apostles from their fishery, and *Matthew* from the receipt of custom; *Amos* from among the herdsmen and *Tekoah*, *Moses* from keeping *Jethro's* sheep, and *Gideon* from the threshing floor, &c. God never encourages idleness, and despises not persons in the meanest employments.

Half the truth is often a great lie.

Prayers and Provender hinder no Journey.

The heathens when they dy'd, went to bed without a candle.

THE THIRTEEN VIRTUES:

1. Temperance: Eat not to dullness. Drink not to elevation.
2. Silence: Speak not but what may benefit others or yourself. Avoid trifling conversation.
3. Order: Let all your things have their places. Let each part of your business have its time.
4. Resolution: Resolve to perform what you ought. Perform without fail what you resolve.
5. Frugality: Make no expense but to do good to others or yourself; i.e., waste nothing.
6. Industry: Lose no time. Be always employed in something useful. Cut off all unnecessary actions.
7. Sincerity: Use no hurtful deceit. Think innocently and justly; if you speak, speak accordingly.
8. Justice: Wrong none by doing injuries or omitting the benefits that are your duty.
9. Moderation: Avoid extremes. Forbear resenting injuries so much as you think they deserve.
10. Cleanliness: Tolerate no uncleanliness in body, clothes, or habitation.
11. Tranquility: Be not disturbed at trifles or at accidents common or unavoidable.

12. Chastity: Rarely use venery but for health or offspring—never to dullness, weakness, or the injury of your own or another's peace or reputation.
13. Humility: Imitate Jesus and Socrates.

Great pride and meanness sure are near ally'd;
Or thin partitions do their bounds divide.

The painful Preacher, like a candle light,
Consumes himself in giving others Light.

Sound, & sound Doctrine, may pass through a Ram's Horn, and a Preacher, without straightening the one, or amending the other.

Different Sects like different clocks, may be all near the matter, 'tho they don't quite agree.

Sin is not hurtful because it is forbidden, but it is forbidden because it is hurtful. Nor is a duty beneficial because it is commanded, but it is commanded because it is beneficial.

Fear God, and your Enemies will fear you.

What is Serving God? 'Tis doing Good to Man.

In the Affairs of this World Men are saved, not by Faith, but by the Want of it.

God, Parents, and Instructors, can never be requited.

Many Princes sin with David, but few repent with him.

Keep thou from the opportunity, and God will keep thee from the sin.

Seek Virtue, and of that possest, to Providence resign the rest.

E'er you remark another's sin, bid your own conscience look within.

Christianity commands us to pass by injuries; policy, to let them pass by us.

Eyes and priests bear no jests.

Danger is Sauce for Prayers.

The Bell calls others to Church, but itself never minds the Sermon.

Many have quarrel'd about Religion, that never practised it.

More carefully the holy book survey:
Your rule is, you should *watch* as well as *pray*.

The end of Passion is the beginning of Repentance.

No resolution of repenting hereafter, can be sincere.

The devil sweetens poison with honey.

The way to see by *faith*, is to shut the Eye of *Reason*: the morning daylight appears plainer when you put out your candle.

To God we owe fear and love; to our neighbours justice and charity; to our selves prudence and sobriety.

Virtue and happiness are mother and daughter.

Doing an Injury puts you below your Enemy;
Revenging one makes you but even with him;
Forgiving it sets you above him.

Vice knows she's ugly, so puts on her Mask.

What more valuable than Gold? Diamonds. Than
Diamonds? Virtue.

With the old Almanack and the old Year,
Leave thy old Vices, tho' ever so dear.

To err is human, to repent divine; to persist devilish.

Search others for their virtues, thyself only for thy
vices.

Each year one vicious habit rooted out, in time might
make the worse man good throughout.

Clean your Finger, before you point at my Spots.

Fear to do ill, and you need fear nought else.

Who is strong? He that can conquer his bad Habits.

Tho' Modesty is a Virtue, Bashfulness is a Vice.

Sloth and silence are a fool's virtues.

If thou injurest conscience, it will have its revenge on thee.

Pride dines upon Vanity, sups on Contempt.

It is better to take many injuries, than to give one.

The excellency of hogs is—fatness; of men—virtue.

'Tis more noble to forgive, and more manly to despise, than to revenge an Injury.

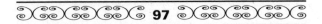

Nothing so popular as goodness.

A true great Man will neither trample on a worm nor sneak to an Emperor.

A long Life may not be good enough, but a good Life is long enough.

He that doth what he should not, shall feel what he would not.

He is a Governor that governs his Passions, and he a Servant that serves them.

Virtue may not always make a Face handsome, but Vice will certainly make it ugly.

Pride gets into the Coach, and Shame mounts behind.

Much Virtue in Herbs, little in Men.

To be proud of Virtue, is to poison yourself with the Antidote.

A Cypher and Humility make the other Figures & Virtues of tenfold Value.

Be at War with your Vices, at Peace with your Neighbours, and let every New-Year find you a better Man.

Without justice courage is weak.

A good man is seldom uneasie, an ill one never easie.

Don't value a man for the quality he is of, but for the qualities he possesses.

A wicked hero will turn his back to an innocent coward.

Keep flax from fire, youth from gaming.

Deny self for self's sake.

The sun never repents of the good he does, nor does he ever demand a recompence.

None preaches better than the ant, and she says nothing.

The noblest question in the world is, *What good may I do in it?*

Hast thou virtue? Acquire also the graces and beauties of virtue.

Let thy vices die before thee.

As often as we do good, we sacrifice.

Vanity backbites more than *malice*.

When you're good to others, you are best to your self.

Sorrow is good for nothing but sin.

Talking against religion is unchaining a tyger; the beast let loose may worry his deliverer.

'Tis not a holiday that's not kept holy.

Generous minds are all of kin.

Meanness is the parent of insolence.

Keep Conscience clear, then never fear.

How many observe Christ's Birth-day; How few his Precepts! O, 'tis easier to keep Holidays than Commandments.

A quiet conscience sleeps in Thunder,
But Rest and Guilt live far asunder.

ON WISDOM AND LEARNING

The wise Man draws more Advantage from his Enemies, than the Fool from his Friends.

The cunning man steals a horse, the wise man lets him alone.

Learn of the skillfull: he that teaches himself, hath a fool for his master.

He that can compose himself, is wiser than he that composes books.

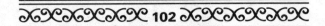

Wise men learn by others' harms; fools by their own.

Experience keeps a dear school, yet Fools will learn in no other.

If what most men admire they would despise,
'Twould look as if mankind were growing wise.

The most exquisite Folly is made of Wisdom spun too fine.

To-morrow I'll reform, the fool does say;
To-day itself's too late;—the *wise* did yesterday.

Genius without Education is like Silver in the Mine.

Tim was so learned, that he could name a Horse in nine Languages. So ignorant, that he bought a Cow to ride on.

He's a fool that cannot conceal his Wisdom.

Fools make feasts and wise men eat them.

The Things which hurt, instruct.

The heart of the fool is in his mouth, but the mouth of the wise man is in his heart.

He that won't be counsell'd, can't be help'd.

It is wise not to seek a Secret and Honest not to reveal it.

The learned Fool writes his Nonsense in better Language than the unlearned; but still 'tis Nonsense.

A learned Blockhead is a greater Blockhead than an ignorant one.

The first Degree of Folly, is to conceit one's self wise; the second to profess it; the third to despise Counsel.

Learning, whether speculative or practical, is, in popular or mixt governments, the natural source of wealth and honour.

The ancients tell us what is best; but we must learn of the moderns what is fittest.

The Wise and Brave dares own that he was wrong.

Write with the learned, pronounce with the vulgar.

Fools need Advice most, but only wise Men are the better for it.

Silence is not always a Sign of Wisdom, but Babbling is ever a Folly.

Liberality is not giving much, but giving wisely.

Wise Men learn by others' harms; Fools by their own.

Life with Fools consists in Drinking;
With the wise Man, living's Thinking.

The doors of Wisdom are never shut.

Being ignorant is not so much a Shame, as being unwilling to learn.

In escaping from a Fire, a Woman, or an Enemy, the wise man will walk, not run.

A taught horse, and a woman to teach, and teachers practising what they preach.

He that knows nothing of it, may by chance be a prophet, while the wisest that is may happen to miss.

Of learned fools I have seen ten times ten; of unlearned wise men, I have seen a hundred.

If thou hast wit and learning, add to it wisdom and modesty.

Most of the learning in use, is of no great use.

He that can bear a reproof, and mend by it, if he is not wise, is in a fair way of being so.

The brave and the wise can both pity and excuse; when cowards and fools shew no mercy.

Proud modern learning despises the antient: *school-men* are now laught at by *school-boys*.

IN VERSE

Take this remark from Richard, poor and lame,
Whate'er's begun in Anger, ends in Shame.

Bright as the day and as the morning fair,
Such Cloe is, and common as the air.

Certainly these things agree, the priest, the lawyer
    and death, all three;
Death takes both the weak and the strong,
The lawyer takes from both right and wrong,
And the priest from the living and dead has his fee.

There's many men forget their proper station
And still meddling with the administration
Of government; that's wrong and this is right,
And such a law is out of reason quite;
Thus, spending too much thought on state affairs,
The business is neglected, which is theirs.
So some fond traveller gazing at the stars,
Slips in next ditch, and gets a dirty arse.
Ye Party Zealots, thus it fares with you,
When Party Rage too warmly you pursue;
Both Sides club Nonsense and impetuous Pride,
And *Folly* joins when *Sentiments* divide.
You vent your Spleen as Monkeys when they pass,
Scratch at the mimic Monkey in the Glass,
While both are *one*; and henceforth be it known,
Fools of both Sides shall stand as Fools alone.

Altho' thy teacher act not as he preaches,
Yet ne'ertheless, if good, do what he teaches;
Good counsel, failing men may give, for why,
He that's aground knows where the shoal doth lie.

My old friend Berryman often, when alive,
Taught others thrift, himself could never thrive:
Thus like the whetstone, many men are wont
To sharpen others while themselves are blunt.

You say you'll spend five hundred pound,
The world and men to know,
And take a tour all Europe round,
Improving as you go.

Dear *Sam*, in search of other's sense,
Discover not your own;
But wisely double the expense,
That you may pass unknown.

Lalus who loves to hear himself discourse,
Keeps talking still as if he frantick were,
And tho' himself might no where hear a worse,
Yet he no other but himself will hear.
Stop not his mouth, if he be troublesome,
But stop his ears, and then the man is dumb.

Against Diseases here, the strongest Fence,
Is the defensive Virtue, Abstinence.
If thou dost ill, the joy fades, not the pains;
If well, the pain doth fade, the joy remains.

Harry Smatter, has a Mouth for every Matter.

My love and I for kisses play'd,
She would keep stakes, I was content,
But when I won, she would be paid,

This made me ask her what she meant:
Quoth she, since you are in this wrangling vein
Here take your kisses, give me mine again.

Dorothy would with John be married;
Dorothy's wise, I trow:
But John by no means Dorothy will wed;
John's the wiser of the two.

Think, bright *Florella*, when you see,
The constant changes of the year,
That nothing is from ruin free,
The gayest things must disappear.
Think of your beauties in their bloom,
The spring of sprightly youth improve;
For cruel age, alas, will come,
And then 'twill be too late to love.

Whate'er's desired, knowledge, fame, or pelf,
Not one will change his neighbour with himself;
The learn'd are happy nature to explore,
The fool is happy that he knows no more.
The rich are happy in the plenty given;
The poor contents him with the care of heaven.
Thus does some comfort ev'ry state attend,
And pride's bestowed on all, a common friend.

I never saw an oft-transplanted tree,
Nor yet an oft-removèd family,
That throve so well as those that settled be.

Observe old *Vellum*; he praises former times, as if he'd
a mind to sell 'em.

To-morrow you'll reform, you always cry;
In what far country does this morrow lie,
That 'tis so mighty long ere it arrive?
Beyond the *Indies* does this morrow live?
'Tis so far-fetched, this morrow, that I fear
'Twill be both very old and very dear.

On his death bed poor Lubin lies;
His spouse is in despair;
With frequent sobs, and mutual cries
They both express their care.
A diff'rent cause, says parson *Sly*,
The same effect may give,
Poor *Lubin* fears that he shall die;
His wife—that he may live.

A lawyer being sick, and extream ill,
Was moved by his friends to make his will,
Which soon he did, gave all the wealth he had,
To frantic persons, lunatick and mad.
And to his friends this reason did reveal,

(That they might see with equity he'd deal,)
From madmen's hands I did my wealth receive,
Therefore that wealth to madmen's hands I leave.
Whimsical *Will* once fancy'd he was ill,

The Doctor call'd, who thus examin'd *Will*;
How is your appetite? O, as to that
I eat quite heartily, you see I'm fat;
How is your sleep anights? 'Tis sound and good;
I eat, drink, sleep, as well as e'er I cou'd.
Will, says the doctor, clapping on his hat,
I'll give you something shall remove all that.

Enrag'd was Buckram, when his wife he beat,
That she'd so often, "lousy knave" repeat.
At length he seized and dragg'd her to the well,
I'll cool thy tongue, or I'll thy courage quell.
Ducking, thy case, poor Buckram, little mends;
She had her lesson at her fingers' ends.
Sows'd over head, her arms she raises high;
And cracking nails the want of tongue supply.

George came to the crown without striking a blow;
Ah!—quoth the Pretender, would I could do so.

William, because his wife was something ill,
Uncertain in her health, indifferent still,
He turn'd her out of doors, without reply:

I ask'd if he that act could justify.
In sickness and in health, says he, I am bound
To keep her; when she's worse or better found,
I'll take her in again, and now you'll see,
She'll quickly either mend or end, says he.

ON T. T. WHO DESTROYED HIS LANDLORD'S FINE WOOD

Indulgent nature to each kind bestows
A secret instinct to discern its foes:
The goose, a silly bird, avoids the fox;
Lambs fly from wolves; and sailors steer from rocks;
A rogue the gallows, as his fate, foresees,
And bears the like antipathy to trees.
Boy, bring a bowl of china here,
Fill it with water cool and clear;
Decanter with Jamaica ripe,
And spoon of silver, clean and bright,
Sugar twice-fin'd in pieces cut,
Knife, sieve, and glass in order put,
Bring forth the fragrant fruit, and then
We're happy till the clock strikes ten.

When painful Colin in his grave was laid,
His mournful wife this lamentation made:
I've lost, alas! (poor wretch, what must I do?)
The best of friends and best of husbands, too.
Thus of all joy and happiness bereft:

And with the charge of ten good children left;
A greater grief no woman sure can know.
Who (with ten children)—*who* will have me now?

Impudent *Jack*, who now lives by his shifts,
Borrowing of driblets, boldly begging gifts,
For twenty shillings lent him t'other day,
(By one who ne'er expected he would pay,)
On his friend's paper fain a note wou'd write.
His friend, as needless, did refuse it quite;
Paper was scarce, and 'twas too hard, it's true,
To part with cash, and lose his paper too.

Things that are bitterer than gall,
Physicians say are always physical:
Now women's tongues if into powder beaten,
May in a potion or a pill be eaten,
And as there's nought more bitter, I do muse,
That women's tongues in physick they ne'er use.
Myself and others who lead restless lives,
Would spare that bitter member of our wives.

Dick's wife was sick, and pos'd the doctors' skill,
Who differ'd how to cure th'inveterate ill.
Purging the one prescribed. No, quoth another,
That will do neither good nor harm, my brother,
Bleeding's the only way. 'Twas quick reply'd,

That's certain death; but e'en let Dick decide.
"I've no great skill," quo' Richard, *"by the Rood,*
But I think bleeding's like to do most good."

Women are books, and men the readers be,
Who sometimes in those books erratas see;
Yet oft the reader's raptured with each line,
Fair print and paper, fraught with sense divine;
Tho' some, neglectful, seldom care to read,
And faithful wives no more than bibles heed.
Are women books? says Hodge, then would mine were
An Almanack, to change her every year.

Grief often treads upon the heels of pleasure,
Marry'd in haste, we oft repent at leisure;
Some by experience find these words misplaced,
Marry'd at leisure, they repent in haste.

When Robin now three days had married been,
And all his friends and neighbors gave him joy,
This question of his wife he askèd then,
Why till her marriage day she proved so coy?
Indeed, said he, 'twas well thou didst not yield,
For doubtless then my purpose was to leave thee.
O, sir, I once before was so beguil'd,
And was resolved the next should not deceive me.
Wedlock, as old men note, hath likened been
Unto a public crowd or common rout;

Where those that are without would fain get in,
And those that are within, would fain get out.

Among the Divines there has been much Debate,
Concerning the World in its ancient Estate;
Some say 'twas once good, but now is grown bad,
Some say 'tis reform'd of the Faults it once had:
I say 'tis the best World, this that we now live in,
Either to lend, or to spend, or to give in;
But to borrow, to beg, or to get a Man's own,
It is the worst World that ever was known.

Says *George* to *William*, Neighbor, have a care,
Touch not that tree—'tis sacred to despair;
Two wives I had, but, ah! that joy is past!
Who breath'd upon those fatal boughs their last.
The best in all the row, without dispute,
Says *Will*—Would mine but bear such precious fruit!
When next you prune your orchard, save for me

(*I have a spouse*) one cyon of that tree.
Deaf, giddy, helpless, left alone,
To all my friends a burthen grown,
No more I hear a great church bell,
Than if it rung out for my knell:
At thunder now no more I start,
Than at the whispering of a fart:
Nay what's incredible, alack!
I hardly hear my *Bridget's* clack.

Good Death, said a Woman, for once be so kind
To take me, and leave my dear Husband behind;
But when Death appear'd with a sour Grimace,
The Woman was dash'd at his thin hatchet Face;
So she made him a Court'sy, and modestly sed,
If you come for my Husband, he lies there in Bed.

Sam's wife provok'd him once; he broke her crown:
The surgeon's bill amounted to five pounds;
This blow (she brags) has cost my husband dear,
He'll ne'er strike more: Sam chanc'd to overhear.
Therefore, before his wife the bills he pays,
And to the surgeon in her hearing says:
Doctor, you charge five pound, here e'en take ten,
My wife may chance to want your help again.

From a cross neighbour, and a sullen wife,
A pointless needle, and a broken knife;
From suretyship, and from an empty purse,
A smoaky chimney and a jolting horse;
From a dull razor, and an aking head;
From a bad conscience, and a buggy bed,
A blow upon the elbow and the knee;
From each of these, good Lord, deliver me.

Some of our sparks to London town do go,
Fashions to see, and learn the world to know;

Who at return have nought but these to show:
New wig above, and new disease below.
Thus the jack-ass, a traveller once would be,
And roam'd abroad new fashions for to see;
But home returned, fashions he had none,
Only his mane and tail were larger grown.

ON BUYING A BIBLE

'Tis but a Folly to rejoice, or boast,
How small a Price thy well bought Purchase cost.
Until thy Death, thou shalt not fully know
Whether it was a Pennyworth or no;
And, at that time, believe me 'twill appear
Extreamly cheap, or else extreamly dear.

Nigh neighbour to the squire, poor Sam complain'd
Of frequent wrongs, but no amends he gain'd.
Each day his gates thrown down; his fences broke;
And injur'd still the more, the more he spoke;
At last, resolv'd his potent foe to awe,
A suit against him he began in law;
Nine happy terms thro' all the forms he run,
Obtain'd his cause—had costs—and was *undone*.

A Parrot is for Prating priz'd,
But prattling Women are despis'd;

She who attacks another's Honour
Draws every living Thing upon her.
Think, Madam, when you stretch your Lungs,
That all your Neighbors too have Tongues;
One Slander fifty will beget;
The World with Interest pays the Debt.

ON THE FLORIDA WAR

From *Georgia* to *Augustine* the General goes:
From *Augustine* to *Georgia* comes our Foes;
Hardy from *Charleston* to *St. Simons* hies,
Again from thence to *Charleston* back he flies.
Forth from *St. Simons* the *Spaniards* creep;
Say, Children, Is not this your Play, *Bo Peep*?

From bad Health, bad Conscience & Parties'
    dull Strife
From an insolent Friend, & a termagant Wife,
From the Kindred of such (on one Side or t'other)
Who most wisely delight in plaguing each other;
From the Wretch who can cant, while he Mischief
    designs,
From old rotten Mills, bank'd Meadows & Mines;
From Curses like these if kind Heav'n defends me,
I'll never complain of the Fortune it sends me.

Ill thrives that hapless family that shows
A cock that's silent, and a hen that crows:
I know not which lives more unnatural lives,
Obeying husbands, or commanding wives.
Doris a widow past her prime,
Her spouse long dead, her wailing doubles;
Her real griefs increase by time;
What might abate, improves her troubles.
Those pangs her prudent hopes supprest,
Impatient now she cannot smother,
How should the helpless woman rest?
One's gone;—nor can she get another.

EVERY MAN FOR HIMSELF, ETC.

A Town fear'd a Siege, and held Consultation,
What was the best Method of Fortification:
A grave skilful Mason declar'd his Opinion,
That nothing but Stone could secure the Dominion.
A Carpenter said, Tho' that was well spoke
Yet he'd rather advise to defend it with Oak.
A Tanner much wiser than both these together,
Cry'd, *Try what you please, but nothing's like
    Leather.*

Giles Jolt, as sleeping in his cart he lay,
Some pilfering villains stole his team away;
Giles wakes and cries,—what's here? a dickens, what?

Why, how?—Am I Giles or am I not?
If he, I've lost six geldings, to my smart;
If not, odds buddikins, I've found a cart.

Two or three frolicks abroad in sweet May,
Two or three civil things said by the way,
Two or three languishes, two or three sighs,
Two or three *bless me's and let me die's*!
Two or three squeezes, and two or three towzes,
With two or three hundred pound spent at their houses,
Can never fail cuckolding two or three spouses.

Syl. dreamt that bury'd in his fellow clay,
Close by a common beggar's side he lay:
And, as so mean a neighbour shock'd his pride,
Thus, like a corpse of consequence, he cry'd;
Scoundrel, begone; and hence forth touch me not:
More manners learn; and, at a distance, rot.
How, scoundrel, in a haughtier tone cry'd he;
Proud lump of dirt, I scorn thy words and thee:
Here all are equal; now thy case is mine;
This is my rotting place, and that is thine.

Kind Katherine to her husband kiss'd these words,
"Mine own sweet Will, how dearly I love thee!"
If true (quoth Will) the world no such affords.
And that it's true I durst his warrant be:
For ne'er heard I of woman good or ill,
But always loved best, her own sweet Will.

As honest *Hodge* the Farmer sow'd his Field,
Chear'd with the Hope of future gain 'twould yield,
Two upstart Jacks in Office, proud and vain,
Come riding by, and thus insult the Swain:
*You drudge and sweat, and labour here,
    Old Boy,*
But we the Fruit of your hard Toil enjoy.
Belike you may, quoth *Hodge,* and but your Due,
For, Gentlemen, 'tis Hemp I'm sowing now.

Celia's rich Side-board seldom sees the Light,
Clean is her Kitchen, and her Spits are bright;
Her Knives and Spoons, all rang'd in even Rows,
No Hands molest, nor Fingers discompose:
A curious Jack, hung up to please the Eye,
Forever still, whose Flyers never fly:
Her Plates unsully'd shining on the Shelf;
For *Celia* dresses nothing, but *herself.*

When will the miser's chest be full enough?
When will he cease his bags to cram and stuff?
All day he labours and all night contrives,
Providing as if he'd an hundred lives,
While endless care cuts short the common plan.
So have I seen with dropsy swol'n, a man,
Drink and drink more, and still unsatisfied,
Drink till drink drown'd him, yet he thirsty dy'd.

Sam had the worst wife that a man could have,
Proud, lazy sot, could neither get nor save;
Eternal scold she was, and what is worse,
The devil burn three, was her common curse.
Forbear, quoth Sam, that fruitless curse, so common,
He'll not hurt me, who've married his kinswoman.

Our smith of late most wonderfully swore,
That whilst he breathed he would drink no more.
But since, I know his meaning, for I think
He meant he would not breathe while he did drink.

What knowing judgment, or what piercing Eye,
Can Man's mysterious Maze of Falsehood try?
Intriguing Man, of a suspicious Mind,
Max only knows the Cunning of his Kind:
With equal Wit can counter-work his Foes,
And Art with Art, and Fraud with Fraud oppose.
Then heed ye Fair, e'er you their Cunning prove,
And think of Treach'ry, while they talk of Love.

Beneath this silent stone is laid,
A noisy, antiquated maid,
Who, from her cradle talk'd till death,
And ne'er before was out of breath.
Whither she's gone we cannot tell;
For if she talks not, she's in Hell!
If she's in Heaven, she's there unblest
Because she hates a place of rest.

A nymph and a swain to *Apollo* once prayed,
The swain had been jilted, the nymph been betray'd;
They came for to try if his oracle knew,
E'er a nymph that was chaste, or a swain that was true.
Apollo stood mute, and had like to be pos'd:
At length he thus sagely the question disclos'd;
He alone may be true in whom none will confide,
And the nymph may be chaste that has never been try'd.

Thus with kind words, squire Edward cheer'd his friend;
Dear *Dick*! thou on my friendship may'st depend;
And be assur'd, I'll ne'er see *Dick* in want.
But now in debt, and all his assets scant,
Dick's soon confin'd,—his friend no doubt would free him:
His word he kept,—in want he ner'er would see him.

Girls, mark my Words; and know, for Men of Sense,
Your strongest Charms are native Innocence.
Shun all deceiving Arts; the Heart that's gain'd
By Craft alone, can ne'er be long retain'd.
Arts on the Mind, like paint upon the Face,
Fright him, that's worth your Love, from your Embrace.
In simple Manners all the Secret lies:
Be kind and virtuous, you'll be blest and wise.

Luke, on his dying Bed, embraced his Wife,
And beg'd one Favour: Swear, my dearest Life,
Swear, if you love me, never more to wed,
Nor take a second Husband to your Bed.
Anne dropt a tear. You know, my dear, says she,
Your least Desires have still been Laws to me;
But from this Oath, I beg you'd me excuse,
For I'm already promised to *John Hughes*.

A farmer once made a Complaint to a Judge,
My Bull, if it please you, Sir, owing a Grudge,
Belike to one of your good Worship's Cattle,
Has slain him out-right in a mortal Battle:
I'm sorry at heart because of the Action,
And want to know how must be made Satisfaction.
Why, you must give me your Bull, that's plain;
Says the Judge, or pay me the Price of the Slain.
But I have mistaken the case, Sir, says *John*,
The dead Bull I talk of, & please you, 's my own:
And yours is that Beast that the mischief has done.
The Judge soon replies with a serious Face:
Say you so? then this Accident *alters the Case*.

All other Goods by Fortune's Hand are giv'n,
A Wife is the peculiar gift of Heav'n.
Vain Fortune's Favours, never at a Stay,
Like empty Shadows, pass, and glide away;
One solid Comfort, our eternal Wife,

Abundantly supplies us all our Life:
This Blessing lasts (if those that try say true)
As long as Heart can wish—and longer too.

A year of Wonders now behold!
Britons despising *Gallic* Gold!
A Year that stops the *Spanish* Plunders!
A Year that they must be Refunders!
A Year that sets our Troops a marching!
A Year secures our Ships from Searching!
A Years that Charity's extended!
A Year that *Whig* and *Tory's* blended!
Amazing Year! that we're defended!

EPITAPH ON A CLERGYMAN

Here lies, who need not here be nam'd,
For Theologic Knowledge fam'd;
Who all the Bible had by rote,
With all the Comments *Calvin* wrote;
Parsons and Jesuits could confute,
Talk Infidels and Quakers mute,
To Every Heretick a foe;
Was he an honest man?—So, so.

My sickly spouse, with many a sigh
Once told me,—*Dicky*, I shall die:

I griev'd, but recollected strait,
'Twas bootless to contend with fate:
So resignation to Heaven's will
Prepar'd me for succeeding ill;
'Twas well it did; for on my life,
'Twas Heaven's will to spare my wife.

Sylvia while young, with ev'ry Grace adorn'd,
Each blooming Youth, and fondest Lover scorn'd:
In years at length arriv'd at Fifty-nine,
She feels Love's Passions as her Charms decline:
Thus Oaks a hundred Winters old
Just as they now expire,
Turn Touchwood, doated, grey and old,
And at each Spark take Fire.

Lord if our days be *few*, why do we spend,
And lavish them to such an evil end?
Or why it be *evil*, do we wrong
Ourselves and thee, in wishing them so long?
Our days decrease, our evils still renew,
We make them *ill*, thou kindly mak'st them *few*.

Some ladies are too beauteous to be wed,
For where's the Man that's worthy of their Bed?
If no Disease reduce her Pride before,
Lavinia will be ravisht at three score.

Then she submits to venture in the Dark,
And nothing now, is wanting—but her spark.

Biblis does Solitude admire,
A wond'rous Lover of the Dark;
Each Night puts out her Chamber Fire,
And only leaves a single Spark;
This, worshipping, she keeps alive—
Warm'd by her Piety, no doubt:
Then, tir'd with kneeling, just at five,
She sighs—and lets that Spark *go out.*

"I give and I devise" (old Euclid said,
And sigh'd) "My Lands and Tenements to Ned."
Your money, Sir? "My money, Sir! what, all?
Why—if I must—(then wept) I give it *Paul.*"
The Manor, Sir? "The Manor! hold," he cry'd;
"Not that—I cannot part with that"—and dy'd.

These Blessings, Reader, may Heav'n grant to thee;
A faithful Friend, equal in Love's degree;
Land fruitful, never conscious of the Curse,
A liberal Heart and never-failing Purse;
A smiling Conscience, a contented mind;
A temp'rate knowledge with true Wisdom join'd;
A life as long as fair, and when expir'd,
A kindly Death, unfear'd as undesir'd.

Your homely face, Flippanta, you disguise
With patch-es, numerous as Argus' eyes:
I own that patching's requisite for you:
For more we're pleas'd, if less your face we view:
Yet I advise, if my advice you'd ask,
Wear but one patch: —but be that patch a mask.

Let no pleasure tempt thee, no profit allure thee, no ambition corrupt thee, no example sway thee, no persuasion move thee, to do any thing which thou knowest to be evil; so shalt thou always live jollily; for a good conscience is a continual Christmas. Adieu.